A LITTLE BOOK OF STAMP COLLECTING

BY

VARIOUS AUTHORS

Copyright © 2013 Read Books Ltd.
This book is copyright and may not be
reproduced or copied in any way without
the express permission of the publisher in writing

British Library Cataloguing-in-Publication Data
A catalogue record for this book is available from the
British Library

Contents

STAMP COLLECTING 1
SOME NEW ISSUES. 5
MORE NEW ISSUES 11
NOTES ON NEW ISSUES 17
NEW ISSUES 23
SOME NEW ISSUES. 29
NOTES AND NEWS. 36
AUSTRALIA AND BACK. 42
A TRAVEL TRIP ROUND EUROPE 46
FROM EUROPE INTO AFRICA 52
MORE MAPS ON STAMPS. 58
AIR STAMPS. 65
SOME CHRISTMAS STAMPS 72
SOME JUBILEE STAMPS TO SAVE. 82
CATALOGUE TERMS 87
ELECTRICITY AS SHOWN ON STAMPS 91
MINERALS ON STAMPS. 98
SUMMER SPORTS ON STAMPS. 105

SPORTS..111

Stamp Collecting

Stamp collecting is the collecting of postage stamps, as well as related objects. It is one of the world's most popular hobbies. Stamp collecting is generally accepted as one of the areas that make up the wider subject of 'philately', which is the study of stamps. A philatelist may, but does not have to, collect stamps – and many casual stamp collectors accumulate stamps for sheer enjoyment and relaxation without worrying about the tiny details. The creation of a large or comprehensive collection, however, generally requires some philatelic knowledge and will usually contain areas of philatelic studies.

Stamp collectors are an important source of income for some countries who create limited runs of elaborate stamps designed mainly to be bought by stamp collectors. The stamps produced by these countries may exceed their postal needs, but may also feature attractive topical designs that many collectors desire. The hobby of stamp collecting began as soon as the first stamps were issued, and by 1860, thousands of collectors and stamp dealers were appearing around the world. The first postage stamp, the 'Penny Black' was issued by Britain in 1840, and pictured a young Queen Victoria. Whilst unused examples of this stamp are quite scarce, used examples are reasonably common, and may be purchased from anywhere from £20 - £200, depending on condition. One of the earliest and most notable stamp collectors was John Edward Gray. In 1862 (only twelve years after stamps were introduced!) he stated that he 'began to collect postage stamps… before it had become a rage.'

As the hobby and study of stamps grew, stamp albums and stamp related literature began to surface, and by the early 1880s publishers like Stanley Gibbons made a business out of this advent. Children and teenagers were early collectors of stamps in the 1860s and 1870s, and most adults dismissed the past time as a childish pursuit. This did not last for long however, as adults began to systematically study the available stamps – and publish books on them. Many stamps have since become legendary; the triangular issues of the Cape of Good Hope, the United States 'Inverted Jenny' (which is actually a printing error' and the Mauritius 'Post Office' stamps – being amongst the best known. Famous stamp collectors include the French / Austrian aristocrat Philipp von Ferray (1850-1917), who at the beginning of the twentieth century, was, and is, widely considered to have collected the most complete stamp assembly ever. It included, for example, all of the rare stamps described above that had been issued by 1917. However, as Ferrary was an Austrian citizen, the collection was broken up and sold by the French government after the First World War, as war reparations. Several European monarchs were also keen stamp collectors, including King George V of the United Kingdom and King Carol II of Romania.

Only a few basic items of equipment are needed to collect stamps. Stamp tongs help to handle stamps safely, a magnifying glass helps in viewing fine details and an album is a convenient way to store stamps. The stamps need to be attached to the pages of the album in some way and stamp hinges are a cheap and simple way to do this, although some collectors prefer more expensive hingeless mounts, if the stamps are valuable. Another alternative is a stockbook where the stamps drop into clear pockets without the need for a mount. Stamps should be stored away from light, heat and moisture or they will be damaged.

Stamp collecting is a less popular hobby now than it was in the early twentieth century, but it is still estimated that about 25 million people enjoy the hobby in the United States, while worldwide the estimated numbers of stamp collectors is around 200 million. There are also thousands of stamp (philatelic) clubs and organizations that provide them with the history and other aspects of stamps. Today, though the number of collectors is somewhat less than in its heyday, stamp collecting is still one of the world's most popular indoor hobbies. Its gentle pleasures, as well as academic interest are enjoyed by individuals all over the world, and it is hoped that the current reader gains the same satisfaction from this work on stamp collecting. Enjoy.

SOME NEW ISSUES

IN the issue of Hobbies dated May 11th, an illustration was given of a Persian stamp, and at the same time readers were reminded of the decree of Persia changing the name to Iran.

This week we illustrate the first Iranian stamp. At least, it seems fair to call it that for up to now the stamps from that country have always had the name Persia. Now, however, they have overprinted some of the 1933 stamps "Postes Iraniennes" so presumably we may expect to find shortly a new issue bearing the latest name. The portrait on this stamp is that of Riza Shah Pahlavi.

From Iron

Manchukuo has just issued four stamps. The 1 1/2 fen and the 6 fen are of the design illustrated while the 3 fen and the 10 fen show two mythical birds—the phoenix. This was a bird which, in Greek Mythology, burneditself in the altar fire, and then arose anew from the ashes. The four stamps were issued to commemorate the visit of Emperor Kangteh to Japan. The illustration, shows Mount Fujiyama which readers may recognise as appearing on some other issues.

From Manchukuo.

TWO British Empire sets have just been issued, in addition to the Jubilee issues, and they are of such merit as deserve careful notice.

The first set is from the Cayman Islands, and two specimens have been selected for illustration. The whole set comprises 12 values 1/4d., 1/2d., 1d., 1 1/2d., 2d., 2 1/2d., 3d., 6d., 1/-, 2/-, 5/-, 10/-. The 1/4d. (and the 3d.) shows a map giving the three islands Grand Cayman, Little Cayman, and Cayman

Brae. The lines of latitude and longitude give definite value to such a map, and in this case the distance between the first and the second gives sufficient space for a portrait of H.M. King George V.

The Cayman Island Turtels.

The other stamp illustrated gives in pictorial manner one of the main products of the Islands—Hawksbill turtles. These turtles, by the way, supply the tortoiseshell of commerce; it is the green turtle which supplies us with the material for soup.

A Map Stamp.

Other designs show a picture of a "cat boat" in the foreground—a boat which appears to have a similar shaped sail to our lug-sail. The 1 1/2d. value is printed vertically and shows a portrait of the King with palm trees on either side and two large shells at the bottom.

The fifth design shows two booby birds, which owe the name to the fact that it allows itself to be caught by hand.

KENYA, Tanganyika and Uganda now issue a combined set of no less than 14 values, so it will be impossible even to describe them all. They are not all of different design, certainly, and here is a description of the two most interesting. The 30 cents printed in blue with the King's head in a circular tablet in black: Below the King's head is the curious double-deck Jinja bridge by the Ripon Falls.

The Ripon Falls are at the north end of Lake Victoria where

the Victoria Nile leaves the lake. This bridge carries a railway above and a twenty foot roadway and two footpaths thirty four feet below the top deck, and cost £30,000 to build. The next bridge down stream over the Nile is at Kosti 1,300 miles to the north, so this one is obviously very important.

The stamp should be a welcome addition to stamp collectors who are also enthusiastic engineering admirers.

A Notable Bridge.

The 65c stamp of the same set has as a central theme—a view of Mt. Kenya, which gives its name to the Colony. It is 17,000 feet high and only a few miles south of the equator. Sir Halford Mackinder first reached the summit, an old volcano, in 1899. At one time it must have been at least 3,000 feet higher.

The shooting round Mt. Kenya is very good and includes

elephant, which accounts for the two fine heads which support the tablet bearing that part of the name 'Kenya & Uganda.'

A Combined Country Stamp.

At the side is a rather curious map of Africa and Europe, and you should notice how different the shape of the land appears from the usual one. This is owing to the designer having placed such a large area in such a small space.

MORE NEW ISSUES

IN the Jubilee Issue of the Philatelic Magazine is a paragraph which should interest readers in explaining one way in which stamps become rare. The writer is sure the editor of that magazine will not object to reference being made to the paragraph in question.

A neighbour was asked to assist an old lady to tidy up her house. In the attic a lot of old Victorian stamps were discovered which had been collected by a deceased member of the family. They consisted of Old Victorian "penny blacks," "two penny blues" and five or six hundred bundles, neatly tied up of the "Mulready" embossed stamp envelopes.

The friend asked the old lady what he was to do with these, and was told to burn the lot as they were only old rubbish. Thus about £500 worth of matter was consigned to the flames! Moral: Before you burn stamps find out what they are worth.

IN these days of very ornate designs it comes somewhat as a surprise to see a plain stamp such as that just issued by Portuguese Guinea, and there is thus very little to describe about this charity stamp. The colour is greenish-yellow, and it is rather large. Perhaps this is as well since it is ungummed—it must be a very messy business sticking a very small stamp on to an envelope by means of gum! The larger size does at least allow one to gum one half and stick that down first then tackle the other half and so keep the fingers clean.

ANOTHER charity issue comes from the Dutch Indies. There are four stamps in this set—2 c. plus 1c., 5c. plus 2 1/2c., 12 1/2c. plus 2 1/2c., and 15c. plus 5c. The designs are different for each stamp, being respectively an engineer chopping wood, a soldier and a wounded man (as illustrated), and a bugler. It is not difficult to understand why the 12 1/2c was picked out as the specimen to be shown.

Lately there have been some very disastrous earthquakes but fortunately nothing as bad as that which happened in 1883 when the volcano Krakatoa in the Dutch East Indies erupted. Then the number of persons killed was 30,000 including those who lost their lives owing to the huge wave which followed.

TURKEY has just issued a set of fifteen stamps in connection with the International Suffrage Congress held at Istanbul. Acknowledgment is made to Messrs. Whitfield King and Co. for this information:—On six of the stamps there are portraits of Nobel Prize winners, while on others are depicted some of the professions adopted by women, and the stamp illustrated shows a school mistress.

Incidently, the geography lesson is presumably on the rivers of South East Europe and the adjacent region of Asia, for the otherwise blank map shows the rivers Danube, Dniester, Dnieper, Volga, Ural, Tigris, Euphrates, and the Nile.

The scene depicted appears to be a very homely affair, and even more so is the next stamp shown, one of an issue of three from Belgium.

These three stamps are of all the same design, and show the children of the King and Queen of the Belgians. The three values are 35c. plus 15c., 70c. plus 30c. and 1fr. 75c. plus 50c., the extra amount being applied to raise funds for the relief of distress among the unemployed in support of an appeal by Queen Astrid. The stamps will be issued until September 30th.

A VERY curious design has been employed by Mexico as

the subject of the 10c. stamp issued in connection with the census. It appears to be a motor tractor with cater pillar wheels forging its way through an enormous cog wheel. In one corner there is a hammer and in the other or opposite is a sickle.

THE last stamp to be illustrated comes from France, and is the 1ft. 50c. stamp issued in connection with the launching of the Normandie. This huge ship is 79,000 tons displacement and 1,027 feet long. You should pace out 342 yards along a road and note the length of that, and only then will you be able to appreciate what an enormous boat this is.

The Normandie was launched on Sunday, May 5th at St. Nazaire.

The pilot was Pilot-Major Serveaux, who is 65 years of age and retires from the French Line after 54 years of service.

NOTES ON NEW ISSUES

THE most interesting set of stamps comes to us this montlrfrom the Philippine Islands. There is a different design for each stamp, but owing to lack of space it is not possible to illustrate each of them in this feature. The 16c. value is picked out because it brings to our notice some of the work of Ferdinand Magellan, who has been previously mentioned on this page.

The Landing of Magellan

This Portuguese explorer was the first man to circumnavigate the globe. Born in 1480 he set sail with a fleet of five ships in an endeavour to reach the East Indies by going south of the American Continent. He set out in August, 1519, reached Patagonia and spent the winter there.

In August, 1520, he recommenced his journey, and passed through the strait which now bears his name. He took three days to go through the rough passage, and when he had passed through, came to the open ocean and calmer water; hence he named this the Pacific. Unfortunately in 1521 he was killed in a fight off the Philippine Islands.

Another interesting specimen from this set shows a view of rice terraces, and possibly at some future date space may be found to illustrate this stamp.

STAMP collectors who are also autograph hunters will have

to obtain two specimens of the stamp from Czecho Slovakia, because that country has just issued a specimen which shows a portrait of President Masaryk and underneath this portrait is to be seen the President's signature.

This appears to be a new departure in stamp designs, and reminds us of the early stamps of The United States of America, for in 1846 Postmaster's Stamps were issued. That is, the Postmasters autographed envelopes before the general government stamps were available and such autographed stamps are to-day valued at up to £3,000. What a pity we did not live in those days and know something of what the value of such stamps would be in the present time!

An Autographed Stamp.

Germany's War Heroes

IN celebration of Germany's War Heroes Day, two stamps have just been issued, and the design on each is the same—that of a German soldier wearing a steel helmet.

At the same time we have a stamp from Switzerland especially overprinted for the use of the Headquarters of the League of Nations. The view on this stamp is that of Mount Pilatus, and is one of the 1934 issue of Switzerland showing views of Switzerland. This is a set which all collectors should try to complete, if only for pictorial merit.

PERSIA, or according to an official decree of last February—Iran—has just issued a set of stamps to commemorate the tenth anniversary of the accession of H.M. Riza Shah Pahlavi. There are nine stamps in the set, but curiously enough the inscription reads Persia and not Iran. Almost as soon as they were issued, however, they were withdrawn, so a fairly rapid advance in price is extremely likely. The specimen of this set chosen for illustration is one which shows the extensive cement works which are situated close to Teheran.

The League of Nations Stamp.

A NOTE from Messrs. Whitfield King & Co., which will be of interest to readers, deals with the issue of high value stamps. No doubt many readers have wondered why such stamps as £1 and £5 values should be needed. Well, New Guinea has found it necessary to issue stamps of such value solely to cope with the transport of gold. All gold is sent from the gold fields by registered mail, and a gold brick contains about 750 ozs. The postage on this is about £20, and to use single pound stamps would be rather like putting wall paper on to a room. Hence the need of high values.

Persian Industries Illustrated

NEW ISSUES

ON the 1st of February 1928, Cyprus issued a set of ten pictorial stamps to commemorate the 50th anniversary of British Rule, and no doubt many readers, of Hobbies Weekly have specimens of this set in their collections. These readers would almost certainly have expressed sorrow on January 31st 1929 when they found that the pictorial stamps were no longer available and that the island had gone back to the old issue, the design of which was the same for all values.

A Cyprus Stamp.

In Memoriam.

Now Cyprus has again come forward with a pictorial set, this time of eleven values with eleven different designs, most of which are ancient monuments.

The stamp chosen to represent this set is the 1 1/2 piastres, and the design shows the Kyrenia Castle and Harbour. A very brief survey of the history of the Island will show the importance of the castle in ancient times. Suppose we start with the coming of Christianity brought to the Island by Barnabas and St. Paul. The prosperity of the island was wrecked by Saracen raids and then later on Byzantine misrule added injury to insult. In 1191 it was occupied by Richard Coeur de Lion and his statue appeared as the main theme on one of the 1928 issue.

The island was then sold to the Templars, and later to the King of Jerusalem whose dynasty gave place to Venetian rule in the latter years of the 15th century. It was during this Venetian rule that Kyrenia Castle was built. The set was issued on December 1st, and on that date the set with the portrait of King George was withdrawn.

LITTLE need be said about the a mourning stamp issued by Jugo-slavia in memory of King Alexandra who was assassinated only a short time ago. There are no less than 14 values in this set, which will probably be on sale for six months. The stamps are all of the same design, similar to that issued in 1931, except there is the black border.

An Unemployment. Stamp.

STAMPS are now used to aid so many various Societies and funds by some countries of the World—that it will not come as a surprise to readers to learn unemployment funds are assisted by this means. Actually this is not the first unemployment stamp which has been issued by Peru. This country in the past had two very appropriately designed stamps for the purpose.

In 1931 and again in 1932.

From Germany.

And the Saar.

Germany was one of the first in the market with her charity stamps and last year she chose to illustrate some of the common ways of earning a living. The set comprises nine stamps ranging from 3 pf. (plus 2 pf. for charity) to 40 pf. (and 35 pf. for charity) and the subjects are as follows; clerk, blacksmith, mason, coal miner, architect, farm labourer, scientist, sculptor, and judge.

Germany seems to be very keen on miners as subjects for stamp designs. These were depicted in the issue of 1921 and again in 1922, and if you compare the issues, the latter appears to be just the reverse of the former.

The Saar Plebiscite which is taking place on Sunday, Jan. 13th, is advertised by overprinting the issue "Volksabstimmung 1935."

The stamps of this territory should be well worth a little extra care. They are not expensive, but the various issues will, in a little while, be of great interest, so collectors should get together a representative collection while the prices are still low.

OFFICE boys seeing the stamp which comes from Cirenaica will be extremely thankful that Great Britain does not go in for such 'posters.' The size of the stamp is 4.8 cms. by 4 cms., while the British 1 1/2d. is only 2.4 cms. by 2 cms., so that it is exactly four times as big. Some idea of the relative size is given in the illustration above, compared with the others.

A Red Cross Stamp.

The last stamp was very kindly sent by Mr. E. Hayes of Romford, and is one of an issue of four from Japan. It was issued in connection with the 15th General Meeting of the Red Cross Society, and shows a view of the building in which the meeting took place.

SOME NEW ISSUES

British Guiana

SINCE the last notes on New Issues, British Guiana has given us an exceedingly picturesque set of thirteen stamps. The 1, 2, and 4c. stamps are almost the same as those of the 1931 issue, with the exception that a portrait of H.M. George V has been added to the 1c. and the dates 1931-1831 have, of course, been removed.

The stamp illustrated is the 6c. which depicts 'Timber logs to be seasoned being shot over falls,' and the 24c. which shows the 'Canes in Punts.'

The complete set with the subjects of the designs is as follows:—1c. Ploughing a Rice Field. 2c. Indian Shooting Fish. 3c. Alluvial Gold Mining. 4c. Kaiteur Falls. 6c As shown. 12c. Stabroek Market Place. 24c. As shown. 48c. Forest Road in Interior. 50c. Same as 4c. 60c. Victoria Regia Lillies. 72. Mount Roraima. 96c. Sir Walter Raleigh and Son. $.Avenue in the Botanic Gardens at Georgetown. The complete list is given because the set is so attractive that full information is well worth having. It is a set which will enhance the look of any album.

Grenada

GRENADA is a small British Island Possession in the Windward Islands-Caribbean Sea about 100 miles to the north of Trinidad, and has an area of only 133 square miles with a population of some 80,000. This country also issued a fresh set which is partly of a pictorial nature, instead of the somewhat drab issue of 1913.

Three stamps the 1/2d., 1 1/2d. and 2 1/2d. are very fine pictorial efforts showing Grand Anse Beach, Grand Etang, and St. George's respectively. The remaining values—we are indebted to Messrs. Whitfield King & Co. for this—consist of two medallions, in one of which is the portrait of the King and the other has the Arms of the Colony. The ten stamps are of the values: 1/2d., 1d., 1 1/2d., 2d., 2 1/2d., 3d., 6d., 1/-, 2/6 and 5/-.

The Argentine

IN May, 1932, the Irish Free State issued two stamps in connection with the International Eucharistic Congress which in that year was held in Ireland.

Now Argentina has given us two in connection with the 32nd Congress which, this year was held at Buenos Aires. The 10c. is illustrated and the design represents a statue of Jesus

Christ holding a Cross. In the background can be seen the Andes and by the side of the Cross appear the words meaning 'Christ, Redeemer of the Andes.'

The 15c. shows a view of the cathedral at Buenos Aires and is a stamp which those who are keen on architecture should try hard to obtain.

Rumania

NO doubtmost people remember the very extensive 'Eat more Fruit' campaign which raged in England a short time ago; well Rumania has been having just such a push lately, the actual dates, as shown on the stamps, being September 14th to 21st, and to further the efforts of those concerned, two stamps have been issued.

The 1 leu shows a picture of a little girl eagerly awaiting

for some grapes to fall into her mouth, but she seems to be holding her hands in case some should not find the right route. The other, the 2 lei, shows a young lady holding a tray containing enough fruit to make anyone ill should they eat it all at once. The two side panels depict even more! The 1 leu is the more attractive because it is clearer.

Bulgaria

BULGARIA has just issued a set of stamps to commemorate the unveiling of a memorial to those who fell in war something like fifty years ago!

In the Balkan Mountains there is a pass which takes the road from Rumelia to Adrianople. It is called the Shipka Pass, and it was here that the fighting took place, where at one time the defenders ran out of ammunition and they used stones as missiles. The first of the set of six stamps has this incident as the theme for the design, and is illustrated.

The U.S.A

THE last stamp chosen for illustration is one of a very beautiful issue of the United States of America, and shows a view of the Yosemite National Park, a beautiful valley of East Central California, U.S.A. It was opened as a National Park in 1890 with an area of 1,162 square miles roughly the area of an English County (Staff-ordshire is 1,128 square miles).

It is rocky and wooded, with unusually big trees.

NOTES AND NEWS

A Useful Gadget

AN exceedingly useful philatelic accessory has been placed on the market by Messrs. Stanley Gibbons called the Thirkell Position Finder. As is the case with most useful things, it is simple and consists of a piece of transparent material with a number of lines drawn at right angles to one another. The horizontal spaces are lettered from A to T, and the vertical spaces numbered from 1 to 17.

By placing a stamp at the top left-hand corner so the outside lines of the Position Finder are touching the outermost edges of the design of the stamp, it is an easy matter to indicate any particular part of the stamp.

Take, as an example, the stamp which, for the purpose of illustration, is fixed behind the finder. It is not too much to ask anyone to find a flaw in, say a part of the sail which comes in the squares D 5 and 6. Without such an accessory it is not at all easy to indicate such a fault unless both parties know the names of the various sails; and in these days of steamships, there are few people who possess such a knowledge.

A Warning

SOME readers may come across a stamp from the United States of America which shows two mallard ducks in flight. The stamp is a large one, being about the size of a Special Delivery Stamp. These stamps are sold at one dollar each and must be affixed to every hunting licence before such a licence is valid.

The stamp is bought at the post office in the usual way, and the proceeds from the sale are devoted to the protection of the water fowl.

It seems a very excellent scheme, and the cause is, no doubt, a worthy one, but the unfortunate part is that the stamps may be bought by anyone. Those who do not intend that they should be used for the proper purpose, have only to sign a contract to say that it will not be used on a hunting licence.

Consequently, we may find these labels which have the appearance of postage stamps, coming on to the market. They have no value for the philatelist and should not be collected.

A Famous Picture

THE stamp illustrated from Spain was issued in June 1930 as one of a set of 'Goya' Commemorative stamps. It depicts

Francisco Goya's famous picture 'The Nude Beauty' and has lately achieved special interest because an old controversy has again arisen, whether the Duchess of Alba is the lady depicted.

There is apparently in the original a certain awkwardness in the position of the head, and a difference in the features between this picture and another portrait of the Duchess which was done by Goya. Consequently, a suggestion has been made that Goya, after painting 'The Nude Beauty' obliterated the face of the Duchess and painted in that of someone else. Other critics have advanced the opposite theory, namely, that the model was some other lady and that Goya painted in the face of his patron.

In order to prove the question one way or the other X ray photographs were taken, but the results when they were examined by experts did not show any indication of one face being painted over the other.

The Design of Stamps

HAVE you ever considered how or why a certain design came to be used for a certain stamp? Of course, sometimes the reason is obvious. For example, certain commemorative issues must have a definite theme incorporated in the design, or in the case of those stamps which are issued when a great man dies.

Such are easy to design, because in each case the central part is decided, and the background must be simple so it does not detract from the most important part.

One point which may not have been noticed by some collectors, is that no stamp of a Crown Colony bears any other portrait than that of His Majesty. This is in accordance with the practice of the Colonial Office of not showing any other identifiable person. Of course, one frequently sees natives depicted, but it would be most difficult to say that any given person was the model.

As an example of how stamps obtain their designs, the case of British East Africa may be quoted. A little while ago it was decided that there should be one issue for Kenya, Uganda and Tanganyika. A competition was made up, and certain rules were laid down for the guidance of the competitors.

The rules stipulated that the design must embody a portrait of His Majesty; it must contain the words "Kenya, Uganda and Tanganyika"; and be of a proportion which could be reduced so the finished stamp should be within certain limits as to size.

AUSTRALIA AND BACK

THIS week we illustrate two items especially collected for "Hobbies" readers, and both have done the journey between England and Australia by air. The first was very thoughtfully sent by a reader, Mr. C. M. Smith of Sydney, for the benefit of other readers, and in order that you should have the illustrations, he sent it by air mail. To quote from Mr. Smith's letter—"The stamps were issued on March 18th in two denominations, the 2d. red and the 1/- black, to commemorate the 20th anniversary of Anzac Day. The design was suggested by the Returned Soldiers League, and contains a representation of the Cenotaph at Whitehall, London, embraced by a laurel wreath, and supplemented by two tilted shields. The drawing, engraving and printing of the stamps being executed by the Commonwealth Stamp Printing Office."

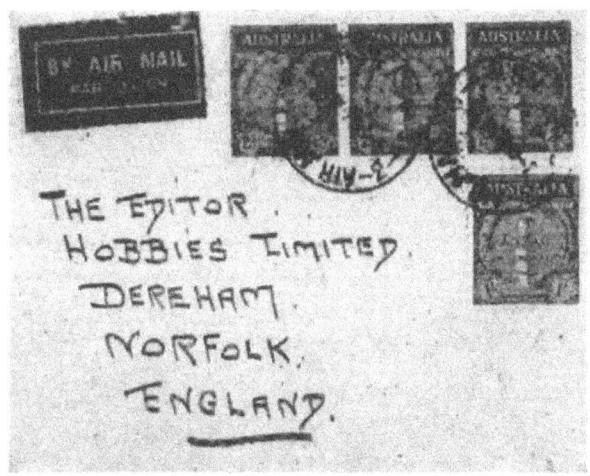

It is exceedingly kind of Mr. Smith to send this envelope, and luckily the postmark has been lightly applied, so that the design is not obscured.

Anzac Day commemorates the landing of the Anzacs at Gallipoli on April 25th, 1915. The word "Anzac" by the way, is formed from the initials of the Australia and New Zealand Army Corps.

THE second illustration shows one of the special souvenir envelopes issued by the Imperial Airways Limited to commemorate the opening of the England to Australia Air mail Service. This service started on December 8th, and this particular envelope was sent out on that date and arrived in Australia in time for Christmas Day.

Their Majesties the King and Queen and His Royal Highness the Prince of Wales sent letters by this mail to the Postmaster General in Australia as souvenirs. The name of the air liner which carried the first mail was the Hengist—though as a matter of fact the mail was so large that two air liners had to set out.

Five and a half years ago the air service between Croydon and Karachi was started and on that occasion about 8,000 letters were sent. But on December 8th last, there were about 100,000 letters, with about 500lbs. of parcels, weighing in all something in the neighbourhood of two tons.

The air mail has by now become such a general matter that normal air letters are of little value. It is only the first flights, or other special letters which are of value. The entire envelope should be kept.

The Garuda Bird

IN one of our pages of Notes, information was asked about the Garuda Bird which appears on the Air stamps of Siam. Mr. A. Murray, of Aberdeen, kindly sends the following interesting note:—

"The design itself is really of religious significance. Brahma was the first God of the Hindu Triad—the Creator in contrast to Vishnu the preserver and Sivu the destroyer. The Garudu, half bird and half man, was the creature upon which Vishnu rode round the world. It is the Garudu which is shown on Siamese stamps, and this bird-man had the head, wings beak and talons of the eagle, and human body and limbs. Its face was white, its wings red, and its body of a golden colour." Our thanks are due to Mr. Murray for his enlightenment.

A TRAVEL TRIP ROUND EUROPE

A Pleasure Trip Round Europe.

A FEW weeks ago we set out on a trip from London to Singapore by Air route, or at least following the air route in the stamp album, and a very interesting trip it made One disadvantage of such a trip is that you have to go along the route on which the Airways Company have already decided what you will see. This week we are going on our own, we shall travel just where fancy takes us, maybe part of the way by boat, perhaps the train may suit us better, though if we are to see everything of interest, then we must employ our legs.

Norway

Denmark

As we are on pleasure bent, let us start towards the north and view that region that so many go to see at midsummer—'The land of the midnight sun.' North Cape is eight or nine degrees north of the Arctic Circle, and is the most northerly point of Europe.

Norway in 1930 issued a set of three stamps showing this point, the three postal values being 15, 20 and 30 ore, they were sold at 40, 45, and 55 ore, the extra amount being given to the Norwegian Tourist Association Fund. There is not much point in journeying further north unless Arctic Exploration is intended, and the route south may be taken by the marvellous Norwegian Fiords, the original home of the Vikings.

On the way south to warmer regions a call at Helsingor in Denmark, on the island of Zealand will recall to our minds that English bard 'William Shakespeare' for the scene of his famous play 'Hamlet' is set at the castle of Kronberg, this castle forms the subject of the design of the 1920 issue from

Denmark. Few English people would go close to this place without making a detour to visit the castle—actually in the play it is called Elsinore.

The journey from the flat country of Denmark may most interestingly be made by boat to Holland and then continue up the river Meuse to Dinant, a little town at the base of very fine cliffs and which is much frequented in Summer by Belgian, Dutch and other visitors, who make this a centre for excursions into the Ardennes.

The 40c stamp of the 1915 issue of Belgium gives an excellent impression of the charm of this spot.

Belgium

A Little Book of Stamp Collecting

Switzerland

Italy

Journeying on in search of more mountain scenery, let us turn to the pages of Switzerland and look at the set issued in 1934 and we have: first a mountain waterfall (Staubbach) then Mt. Pilatus, Grimsel Pass, the Gothard railway, Viamala Gorge, the Rhine waterfall near Schaffhausen, and also the

Castle at Chillon with the Dents du Midi in the background; this last is the one selected for illustration, for it was at the Castle of Chillon that Bonnivard—the defender of Geneva—was kept prisoner for six years by the Duke of Savoy, the tale of which is told by Lord Byron. It seems a pity that these stamps are so small, such marvellous scenery do they portray.

Having gone as far south as Switzerland, one could hardly retrace one's steps without going the little extra distance necessary to visit Italy, and then having reached this country, what a wealth of famous towns from which to choose.

Venice immediately jumps to mind, but then we have passed over many miles of low lying country when we journeyed from Denmark up the Meuse to Dinant, so let us leave Venice and go to Rome and see the largest church in Christendom—St. Peters—with which the names of Raphael and Michaelangelo are associated. St. Peters occupies the site of Caligula's Circus in which Nero tortured the Christians—it covers 18,000 square yards and is 435 ft. high, so large indeed that St. Paul's Cathedral, London, could be re-erected inside it.

Curious land formations are not often adopted as subjects of the design of stamps—beauty spots, high mountains and lakes certainly, but surely the design of the French 90c stamp of 1929-1933 must tempt many people to make the journey to see such formations.

These extinct volcanic craters are distinctive features of the landscape; Le Puy en Velay consists of a new town on the flat land the old town built on the abruptly sloping puy or hill—the streets are so steep as to be impassable for carriages, and the highest point is crowned by a colossal statue of the Virgin, cast from cannon captured at Sebastopol.

France

From Le Puy en Velay let us go to another rock—The Rock of Gibraltar, a view of which is seen on the 1931-1933 stamps of this Crown Colony. This rock is 1,400 ft. high and was secured in 1704 by Sir George Rooke.

FROM EUROPE INTO AFRICA

WHEN we had a pleasure trip through Europe, we finished up at Gibraltar, mainly because this spot should prove an excellent stepping off place for a similar trip through Africa.

It would be very difficult to say which of the continents has provided the most interesting stamps, but certainly Africa would be high up in the list. From a general interest point of view, scenery, animals, native types etc., it would be difficult to beat the stamps from 'The Dark Continent.'

Just across the water from Gibraltar we enter Morocco. The British Protectorate has British stamps overprinted Tangier, but as we pass south we should travel through French territory, visiting the town of Fez, which we see depicted on the 1917 stamp of French Morocco.

The view shown must surely recall P. C. Wren's books and the film 'Beau Geste,' This is only one view; there are others in the set which followed, so that a very good appreciation of the country may be obtained from the pages of" the stamp album.

A Little Book of Stamp Collecting

A complete collection of the stamps of Liberia is a collection well worth seeing. Messrs. Water-low & Sons, Perkins, Bacon & Co., and the American Bank Note Co., have in turn produced perfect pictures of animals, plants and views. Among the animals we may see the elephant, rhinoceros, chimpanzee, plantain-eater, lizard, egret, civet, leopard, alligator, etc., including snakes, the particular specimen illustrated being on a registration stamp from Monrovia. Of the products of the vegetable kingdom illustrated, must be mentioned the fine picture of part of the pepper plant.

Liberia has been an independent Negro Republic since 1847 and has produced many stamps which though they could not be called valuable, are certainly difficult for the average collector to obtain.

JOURNEYING inland we come to the French Dependency Niger—and since Niger territory only came into being in 1921 it is not surprising that there are far fewer stamps. However, one is important as illustrating the manner of obtaining water. The bucket is not let down the well as in England but is fastened to a long pole which acts as a lever. This type of well is in use in other parts of Africa.

Up to 1923 Belgian Congo was issuing stamps giving some very pretty general views such as the Stanley Falls and the Inkissi Falls, but in that year the famous 'Native Type' set was issued from which we can at least see some extraordinary ways of doing hair. In the case of the 5c. value the lady's hair has been soaked in oil in order that it may set in the manner depicted.

The stamp illustrated shows some of the native kraals, notice that the border is made of a design formed from spears and shields, the borders of stamps are frequently most interesting and should be studied just as carefully as the central theme.

In connection with the subject of natives represented on stamps, a most interesting little book has just been brought out by Messrs. Stanley Gibbons of 391 Strand, W.C.2. It is called 'Native Races of the Stamp Album' and it is written by A. E. Gould. It only costs 1/-, but makes some of the curious figures much more interesting.

UNFORTUNATELY we cannot linger any longer in this part of Africa, but must continue on our journey. Sooner or later we shall reach South Africa and the 1933 Voortrekker Monument stamps are particularly interesting on a trip such as we are taking. They commemorate the Great Trek of 1835 when 10,000 people crossed the Orange River.

Three stamps were issued, the 1d. plus 1/2d., the 2d. plus 1d. and the 3d. plus 1 1/2d., the extra being given towards the Voortrekker Monument.

Notice that in this case a pair of stamps has been shown because one has been printed in English—South Africa—and the other in Afrikaans—Suid Afrika—either language will serve us because the country is bilingual. The stamps are printed alternately throughout the sheet, and should be collected in pairs, a pair being worth about three times a single specimen.

Mozambique on the east coast will be our next stop. Here, judging by the set issued in 1918, they must be very busy indeed for no less than twelve industries or commodities are illustrated.

MORE MAPS ON STAMPS

WHEN you tell a person that you are a stamp collector you are very frequently met with the question "Have you any triangular stamps?" Most people who do not enjoy this hobby imagine that Cape triangulars are the most valuable stamps there are. Actually this is not the case, though the cost of most of them is outside the pocket of most of us.

A Lithuanian Triangular.

However, here is a triangular stamp that does not cost

anything like as much as a 'Cape.' In fact it can be purchased for the modest sum of twopence, and the design is far more interesting than the more valuable specimen. It shows a map of the issuing country—Lithuania and the printing of this stamp leads one to believe that Lithuania is almost surrounded by the sea, except on the south east. This is due to the way in which the boundaries of the adjacent countries have been printed, for Lithuania has only a very short coastline and that on the extreme west.

The Costa Rica Republic.

It is worth looking at a good atlas so as to obtain a correct idea of the boundaries of this and of the countries to the north of this relatively new stamp issuing country, new in comparison with the older pre-war countries that is.

The remainder of the stamps which are illustrating this

article come from across the Atlantic, and the first of these shows the gateway to the Pacific. This is a very beautifully engraved stamp, the work being executed by the American Bank Note Company, and will amply repay a few minutes examination with a good magnifying glass.

The Panama Country.

In addition to the valleys which are easily visible, one can see two ships, one entering the canal at Panama, and one leaving at Colon. Now comes one very serious disadvantage from which this stamp suffers. It appears from the engraving that the canal is directly east to west, and since it leads from the Atlantic to the Pacific Ocean the direction seems to be correct.

Actually the canal is cut in a south-west to a north-east direction, and furthermore it must be remembered that

Colon is on the Atlantic side, and Panama on the Pacific. This particular stamp appeared in 1915, though the canal was not officially opened until 1920.

A U.S.A. Purchase.

In 1896 one of the neighbouring countries—Nicaragua—issued a stamp showing a map of their country. On it there is a very large lake, and from the south east corner a river, the San Juan, flows into the Atlantic.

The inhabitants of Nicaragua hoped that the canal would be cut through their country, using the lake and the river as part of the waterway, and this might have happened but for the fact that this is a very volcanic region and people do not like subscribing money to be expended in a place where it may all be lost during a short earthquake.

From Nicaragua.

The next stamp comes from the country situated between these two last. It is from Costa Rica, and was issued in 1924 to commemorate the incorporation of the province of Nicoya—which is the major portion of Guanacaste—into the Republic of Costa Rica. From 1885 to 1890 the people of the province of Guanacaste were allowed to purchase the postage stamps of Costa Rica at twelve per cent. less than face value.

A Confederation Stamp.

The reason for this concession seems to be somewhat obscure, but since Nicaragua was disputing the right of Costa Rica to the possession of Guanacaste one can imagine that it was an endeavour to strengthen the loyalty of the inhabitants of the province to the Republic. The name Guanacaste was overprinted on the stamps which were then only available for use in the named province.

The two other stamps together complete the map of North America, but they also have some very interesting information to impart. The stamp from the U.S.A. was issued in 1904 commemorating not only the International Exhibition at St. Louis, but also the 'Louisiana Purchase.'

The region which is shaded and which has the figures 1803 printed on was in that year purchased by the United States from France for the sum of £3,000,000. The next stamp also commemorates a purchase by the United States, though this is not the reason for its appearance.

It will be noted from this specimen that Alaska is not part of Canada. It was purchased by U.S.A. from Russia in the year 1867, and the price paid was $7,200,000 or £1,450,000. Curiously enough the date of the purchase appears on the stamp, ut the reason for this date being seen is quite different.

It was in 1867 that the Confederation of Canada took place, and the date of issue 1927 is the 60th anniversary of this Confederation.

A second point worthy of note is that Labrador is not shaded in the same way as the rest of Canada. That is because it does not belong to Canada but to Newfoundland.

Lastly, notice the railway line which extends across the stamp. It is there because British Columbia refused to enter the Confederation unless this construction of a fast method of transport was undertaken, so that the railway line is a real symbol of Confederation.

AIR STAMPS

THE first Official Government Air Stamp was issued in 1917, and that was by Italy, some of her express stamps being overprinted for experimental flights between Rome and Turin, and between Naples and Palermo (in the island of Sicily). The first illustration shows one of the former of these stamps.

The First Italian Stamp.

A Little Book of Stamp Collecting

From 1917 to the present day is not a very long time from a philatelic point of view, but it is quite long enough for some of the earlier stamps to have become decidedly valuable. In 1918 The United States of America issued a 24 cent stamp for use on air mail from Washington to Philadelphia, 24c. is roughly 1/- now one of these stamps is worth £800! So an investment of a few shillings in 1918 would have repaid the speculator very well. Unfortunately, we did not think that these stamps would work out like this!

As a matter of fact in this case the stamp was a freak, the aeroplane being printed upside down in error.

We cannot all find these valuable freaks, but fortunately there is a fascination in philately in addition to the chance of finding something good. There appears to be a peculiar fascination in just this one branch of the hobby. Sufficient, in fact, to make some people indulge in aero philately to the exclusion of other branches. There is a club devoted to this side—The Aero-philatelic Club of London.

The Ideas of a Painter!

Other people take it up as a side line to the real collection while others still collect air stamps and put them in the same album as the, shall we call them, 'land and sea' stamps.

There are some very interesting stamps from which one can almost trace the history of flying, and luckily most of these can be obtained quite cheaply. So one may very justly claim that in philately the greatest interest is not confined to those with the longest purse.

The stamp issued in 1932 by Italy shows a picture of Leonardo da Vinci's flying machine. He lived from 1452 to 1519 and is best remembered as an artist. He studied art at Florence, though at the same time he studied mathematics; as an artist he would naturally have a discerning eye, and it seems that his attempts at constructing a flying machine depended on his observations on the flight of birds. From the stamp his machine appears to consist of two huge feathers operated by wires attached to his feet.

Wilbur Wright's Machine.

The next airman to be mentioned here and who appears on stamps is Santos Dumont, he was born in 1873 at Sao Paulo and was the son of a coffee king of Brazil. His first voyage was in 1897 and in 1901 on October 19th (as on the stamp above) he navigated his balloon round the Eiffel Tower, Paris and by so doing won the Deutch prize of 100,000 francs. In 1929 Brazil issued a set of stamps, the 200 reis as shown, the 10,000 reis bearing a portrait of Santos Dumont, while the 500 reis showed his biplane.

Next we come to Wilbur Wright, who was born in 1867 in U.S.A. He improved the gliding machine and put in an engine. He started with a 4-cylinder 12-horse power motor—a contrast with an Imperial Airways liner of to-day with its four engines, each developing 555 horse power. Yet with his 12 h.p. motor he managed to stay in the air for 59 seconds and achieved a speed of 30 miles per hour.

His aeroplane is now in the South Kensington Museum and a picture of it is on the 1928 issue of U.S.A. Two stamps were brought out to commemorate the 25th anniversary of the Wright Brothers first flight.

Mention must be made here of a stamp illustrated a little while ago and described with some other new issues, namely the French Stamp showing Louis Bleriot crossing the Channel.

An Effort from Siam.

All countries are not able to portray a World famous pioneer on their air stamps, and some of the designs can be called weird and wonderful. As an example take the Siamese air stamp shown. The flying object is the mythological 'Garuda Bird,' and perhaps some kind reader can give us further information about this myth? bottom line we see 'U 34'; this is called a Control or a Control Number. Between the sixth and seventh stamps on the bottom line is a mark-.-. The purpose of this is to aid the post office clerk to separate the stamps quickly, so if some one asks for 5/- worth of halfpenny stamps then he does not have to count out 120, but just tear off above the mark and pass the stamps over the counter.

NEXT we come to the line which is printed on the margin. This is called the Jubilee Line. It received this name because sheets showing this line were first printed during the year 1887, the Jubilee year of Queen Victoria.

The purpose of this line is to take the first jar when printing. If there is something which does not really matter taking this first shock, then there is far less danger of the actual stamp printing surface getting damaged. Sometimes this line is unbroken, in which case it is called Continuous. In the case illustrated, the line is broken between each stamp, and this is called Co-Extensive.

Lastly, in connection with this illustration, the margin is whole on the bottom, while on the right it is perforated. When the bottom margin is as in the illustration, then it is given the name Margin Imperforate. When the bottom margin is as on the right, then it receives the name Margin Perforate. Usually these terms are abreviated to marg. imperf. and marg. perf.

A term which is very frequently met with when looking at price lists, advertisements and catalogues is the expression Mint. There are thirty-six 'mint' stamps shown; that is to say that the stamps are all as issued, in perfect condition, clean, and with the gum on the back.

SOME CHRISTMAS STAMPS

EVERY year certain countries of the World issue a stamp or a set of stamps at Christmas-time and generally speaking these stamps are sold at a premium, that is that the purchasers have to pay more for them than is stated on the value tablet, the extra amount going towards some charity.

People usually feel they are glad to help charity at this time of the year, so that they do not mind paying a little extra to send their letters and parcels when they know that the cause is good.

Switzerland is, perhaps, the best known of these countries, for she issued the stamp illustrated in 1913. Swiss Charity Stamps bear the words 'Pro Juventute' indicating that they are used for Child Welfare.

A Little Book of Stamp Collecting

Watches on a Stamp.

A Charity Stamp.

From 1918 to 1926 the designs were composed solely of the arms of tne various cantons or provinces, and though these do not sound as though they would be very interesting yet they have very curious side panels which are well worth studying. The second stamp illustrated was issued in 1923 and shows the arms of Neuchatel as the main theme, while watches are to be seen forming the sides.

Very possibly some of you will be wanting a new watch—here is the stamp to go with it. The arms series was dropped for 1927 but three more appeared in 1928 and another in 1930.

The third illustration is one of the four charity stamps issued last year, three values of which show very lovely portraits of maidens. One is taken from Vaud on the 5c, that on the 10c. is a Bernese maiden, while on the 20c. one sees a Tessinese. The other stamp of this issue bears a portrait of G. Girard.

Unfortunately, these Swiss stamps are only issued on December 1st so it is impossible to illustrate this year's set at the moment, but if the designs are sufficiently interesting, they shall appear in a later issue of Hobbies Weekly.

A Dutch Theme.

The stamps which come from Holland in the cause of Child Welfare have in the past few years appeared on December 10th. Last year the design was rather effective—the 1 1/2c. represented "A Child and the Star of Epiphany." The designs of previous Christmas stamps, however, have not been so happy.

For instance, those of the 1931 set were as follows: 1 1/2c. a deaf mute; 5c a mentally deficient child, 6c. a blind girl; and the 12 1/2c. a sick child. The values cited do not include the premium, the stamps actually selling at 3c., 8c., 10c. and 16c. respectively.

Mozart illustrated.

Austria annually issues charity stamps, though in this

country the premium varies considerably. For instance in 1922 they had a Musicians set—portraits of Hayden, Mozart (illustrated), Beethoven, Schubert, Bruckner, Strauss, and Wolf appearing on the 2 1/2, 5, 7 1/2, 10, 25, 50, and 100 kr. respectively. The rather remarkable fact about this set was that they were issued at no less than ten times face value. In 1923, Austria charged six times the face value for that year's set, while in 1924 the price went down to four times.

In 1932 the Dutch Indies issued a set of charity stamps, the money raised going to the aid of the Salvation Army. The designs showed (1) natives at work weaving (2) plaiting rattan, (3) textile working and (4) metal working. The 5c. stamp which is illustrated shows a native at work plaiting rattan.

Belgium has also given us a number of very beautiful charity stamps at Christmas-time, and these are in aid of the Anti-tuberculosis Fund. The stamp illustrated is one of the 1930 issue, and represents a view of Ghent Castle. This fine old castle, called the Château des Comtes de Flandre, is almost surrounded by the waters of the Lieve which forms the moat, and dates from 1180, though the castle was founded in the ninth century.

Here it was that the famous John of Gaunt, the son of Edward III was born in 1340. The fine belfry of Bruges is illustrated on the 5fr. stamp of the 1929 Christmas set. Notice the curious cross appearing above the castle which on the 1933 set is called "The Cross of Lorraine."

The Dutch Indies.

There are a number of other countries which have these Charity sets at Christmas-time, but there are also a considerable proportion of the stamps which find their way into the album which remind us, if not of the weather which we have, at least of the weather we associate with this festive season.

Ghent Castle.

Ancient Modern.

Possibly the most "Christmassy" stamp in the album is the 15c. of the 1931 Air Set of Newfoundland, which, as the illustration shows, consists, of an aeroplane flying over a dog team. Ths idea of the stamp is to show the advance in speed with which mails are now carried.

One of the easiest ways of understanding what this means is to take as an example the fact that one can now send a copy of this number of Hobbies Weekly to anywhere on earth provided that it has a postal service—and by using the aeroplane the addressee would get it by Christmas day. By the older method of dog team, it would have been considerably after the New Year before the book would have reached its destination.

Almost everyone would like to see the snow covered countryside as seen in that stamp. Were that so, then the sport shown on the, Unite States of America stamp of 1932 would be very popular. This was issued on the occasion of the Winter Olympic Games at Lake Placid, one of the Saranac Lakes 80 miles south of Montreal, and shows a side that Great Britain has to a great extent to neglect. For although most of us know that the Olympic Games comprise mostof the known sports, yet a number do not realise that Winter Sports come into it.

The Winter Games.

The Falkland Islands.

In fact quite a number of people who do not collect stamps, would be surprised to hear that association football is one of the contests. Stamp collectors know this by the stamp issued by Uruguay, and which was shown in our issue dated October 6th.

Another stamp showing typical Christmas weather (this time on the sea instead of the land) is the copy of the 1d.

1933 issue from the Falkland Isles. This set was issued to commemorate the centenary of British Occupation. This illustration had to come in because it serves two purposes, one to remind us that all kinds of wintry weather are not welcome, and that the other side of the equator is having warm summer weather now. The Falkland Isles are bathed in sunshine, and the icebergs are nearer to them in June than now!

The last stamp also shows some who do not like the cold, and illustrates the hardships entailed to the weary. These stamps were sold at a premium, the extra being given to the benefit of Hungarian prisoners of war in Siberia.

The Terrors of Winter.

These Stamp articles are a regular intersting feature.

SOME JUBILEE STAMPS TO SAVE

ONE would like to be able to give illustrations of all the Jubilee stamps from the Dominions, for some of them are exceedingly handsome, but space forbids and so the best thing to do is to pick out some.

The one design which served for all the Crown Colonies has already been shown. If we take the familiar British Jubilee stamp first, we find that this has been overprinted in different ways for use in North Africa. First of all there is the overprint 'Tangier' then again there is a set overprinted 'Morocco Agencies,' the values being left as in the British currency. Another overprint is 'Morocco Agencies' at the sides with the value in French currency at the bottom—5, 10, 15, 25 centimes respectively, and lastly the same at the sides but the values in Spanish currency, 5, 10, 15, 25 centimos.

South Africa has produced eight stamps, though there are only four values (the 1/2d., 1d., 3d. and 6d.) because each value has two types. The only difference is that on one stamp the English version of the name 'South Africa' is at the top with the Afrikaans at the bottom, and on the other the position is reversed. As the stamps were printed alternately on the sheet they should be collected in pairs to show the method of printing.

While South Africa in order to overcome the bilingual difficulty issued two stamps for each value, South West Africa overcame the same trouble by placing the English and Afrikaans version on either side of the King's head. The four values in this case being 1d., 2d., 3d. and 6d., the design is the same for each stamp.

A MUCH more pleasing picture was chosen for the four stamps from Southern Rhodesia, 1d., 2d., 3d. and 6d. Readers will no doubt recognise the famous Victoria Falls on the Zambesi river which forms the background, a slightly different view having formed the basis of the design for previous issues.

The choice of portrait of H.M. King George V is also a matter of congratulation, and the giraffe, elephant, lion and springbok are splendidly clear.

Canada produced six Jubilee stamps each having a different portrait or design. It would certainly be very nice to be able to show all six, they are so beautifully clear and pleasing, but space prohibits, so the most unusual is chosen.

The 1c. is a very charming picture of Princess Elizabeth, and on the 2c. the Duke of York figures. The 3c. is perhaps the nearest to the popular idea of the design for a Jubilee stamp having portraits of H.M. George V and H.M. Queen Mary side by side, with the dates in side panels. The Prince of Wales appears on the 5c. and a view of Windsor Castle (not the same view as on the Crown Colonies issue) is shown on the 10c.

The 13c. illustrates the royal yacht "Britannia" and this is a beautiful stamp, with the picture of the famous yacht almost perfect.

The unused set may be purchased for 1/9 and since each design is different, and forms the basis of an excellent Royal Portrait Gallery it should form a worthy addition to any collection.

INDIA went one better than Canada, producing seven stamps, 1/2, 3/4, 1, 1 1/4, 2 1/2, 3 1/2 and 8 annas. The portrait of H.M. King George V and the surround is the same for each, but there is a fairly large panel containing a very fine engraving of various famous Indian buildings.

These, in order of the value on which they appear, are the Gateway of India (Bombay); Victoria Memorial (Calcutta); Rames waram Temple (Madras); Jain Temple (Calcutta); Taj Mahal (Agra); The Golden Temple (Amritsar); and a Pagoda in Mandalay. Here you have an absolute picture gallery of Indian architecture.

CATALOGUE TERMS

EVERYONE who collects stamps should do his or her utmost to procure a stamp catalogue. Without such a reference book it is impossible to arrange a collection properly. Moreover, this book should serve as a basis of comparison when exchanging stamps with other people. The idea of one stamp being given in exchange for one received, is by no means correct. Value must come into the transaction, and the less experienced the collector, the more he needs a catalogue to ensure that he is not being exploited!

What is a stamp catalogue? It is essential to understand this; before it can be used properly. It is simply a book giving the price at which the firm is prepared to supply the stamps listed, provided, of course, they are in stock.

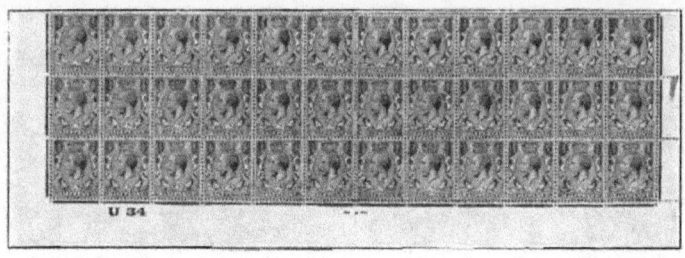

Now if you look at a stamp catalogue you will see that even the most common stamps are listed at one penny, and you will immediately exclaim that the price is too high. From your point of view you are correct, but the dealer has just as much trouble in taking a common stamp out of his stock as he has in taking a more valuable one and the time taken to despatch is exactly the same. So to charge less than one penny for the common stamps would not pay him.

THE reason this is put plainly is because, you should realise that the catalogue must not be used for the purpose of valuing your collection.

If you try to do this then a collection of 500 of the commonest stamps would work out at least 500 pence or £2 1s. 8d. And as you know a packet of 500 different stamps can be purchased for about three shillings.

The catalogue will, however, give you an idea of the relative value of stamps when exchanging. It will also tell you the date of the issue of any particular stamp, and the number of stamps in the set. That information is valuable enough in all conscience, and without, it is impossible to make proper provision for the collection in the album.

There is, however, far more information than this to be gained if one knows something about the catalogue, and it is in order that you may gain this extra information that these notes are given.

Luckily there are so many philatelists in the world that by now the terms are standardized. So there is no risk if you buy one catalogue and your friend buys another that the terms in yours will be different from those in his. Also the values are so nearly the same that differences of opinion are not likely to arise.

THERE are two or three ways in which this explanation of terms may be tackled. One would be to take the terms in alphabetical order and then describe and illustrate as they come along. This would be the best way if one was to take all the terms, but there are quite a number which only the specialist will ever want, so that some will be omitted.

This being the case, the more interesting way will be to take an illustration and then talk about that. If it gives us more than one definition—so much the better, if only one, then we will pass on to the next.

The particular illustrations are taken where possible from relatively common stamps, and one of the best possible ways of thoroughly understanding the terms, is to find other examples in your own collections.

AS a start, examine the illustration of the English halfpenny stamps shown quite a number of terms will be explained from this one illustration.

The thirty-six stamps would be termed a Block. This is the name given to any number of stamps which are joined together, provided that the Block is less than a whole Sheet. A sheet of halfpenny stamps is worth 10/-, which means that it contains 240 stamps, or 20 horizontal Strips of twelve in each, and 12 vertical strips of 20 in each.

There are three such horizontal strips shown and twelve vertical strips of three in each. All round the sheet of stamps there is a Margin.

ELECTRICITY AS SHOWN ON STAMPS

SO many commemorative stamps are now being issued, that one might almost say that they appear daily. Unfortunately, so many have come to us lately, that it is almost impossible to study them all and to derive the interest and benefit that should be available had we the time to take each one and compare it with those which are related to it either by the design or by the event it commemorates.

Take electricity. The saying "familiarity breeds contempt" is very true in this case and thousands of those who press a switch whenever they want to look at their stamp albums, forget what they owe to those who discovered the uses of this force.

The Refrigerating Cengress—Argentine 1932.

The Belguim Exhibition 1930.

It would be only fitting if all those who enjoy the use of electric light, should spend the necessary copper or two and purchase a copy of the stamp commemorating the 50th anniversary of the production (Edison's first electric lamp) issued by the United States of America in 1929. The United States certainly have to thank T. A. Edison, for it was he who set up the first electric supply station in New York in 1881.

The First Electric Motor

A NUMBER of fellows are extraordinarily keen on model railways, spending hours reading up about their hobby. But how many of them can give the information as to who it was who discovered the electric motor? As to what he looked like—well that is too much to ask! Their stamp collecting friends should be able to point out to them the 1926 issue of Belgium, which commemorates the birth of Gramme. It was this man who made the transmission of electric power possible.

San Marino is only a small republic of some 38 square miles, but it has issued a very nice set of stamps bearing a view of an electric train. The line runs from the capital to Riminin, and the stamps were in commemoration of the opening of this line.

If asked where our greatest supplies of meat come from, most people would be able to answer Australia, New Zealand and the Argentine, and for them the matter would end there. Boats take time to traverse such a stretch of ocean as is necessary, and they have to pass through temperatures which would very soon cause meat to go bad were it not for the invention which the Argentine has very deservedly depicted upon one of its stamps issued in connection with the International Refrigerating Congress.

The 50th anniversary of Edison's first electriclamp.

Cold Storage Stamps

Though, perhaps, not altogether electrical yet, the latest meat safes are well known by all. It is not only our meat supply that we owe to this invention, however. The sight of a wreath of fresh flowers sent all the way from Australia to be placed at the foot of the Cenotaph, in Whitehall, will always serve as a reminder of its powers.

Guatemala Wireless Station 1919.

A Little Book of Stamp Collecting

Italy's commemoration of Volta's death.

ITALY gives her contribution, as well as the small republic situated as it were within her boundaries. An issue of a set of four stamps on the occasion of the centenary of the death of Volta. This scientist was born in 1745 and was a professor in Pavia University, he constructed the earliest absolute electrometer, so that he is certainly worthy of a place on the stamps of the world.

No display of stamps concerning electricity could be called anything like complete without showing one depicting wireless. In this case we have quite a wide choice. The clearest view of a wireless station is that on the 1919 issue of Guatemala, the one illustrated. Mention must, however, be made of the 1925 Popov commemoration stamps of Russia, which are inscribed "Inventor of Wireless-Popov."

A Little Book of Stamp Collecting

The San Marino Electric Railway Opening.

A very odd idea for collecting in midget photography is sent in by one of our Austrian readers. A midget photograph is framed by stamps on *one* block and, of course, stamped regularly by the post office. If you find this interesting, our Austrian correspondent says he would be glad to send you one of these stampframed midget views. Write to Mr. ing. Rudolf Trimmel, Wien, X., Laxenburgerstraze 26, Austria. Please write clearly and don't forget to mention Hobbies Weekly.

A POSTCARD

Will bring you a free copy of this interesting publication,

AIR MAIL LIST No. 4

New edition just published. Offers an immense variety of air stamps. First Flight and other fascinating flown covers.

Write for it now.

WHITFIELD KING & CO.,   IPSWICH

                                Suffolk

Established 1869.

MINERALS ON STAMPS

TWO of the stamps illustrated this week require very careful scrutiny if the design is to be understood. Both of these come from South America. One of the designs is symbolical, and the best clue that we have as to what it is meant to represent is the ear of wheat which figures at each side of the stamp.

It is one of a set of stamps issued to commemorate the exporting of the first cargo of Chilian nitrate. The two other stamps of the same set show a man spreading artificial manure, and as the man appears to be scattering manure all over the world, no doubt Chili would like to send its produce everywhere.

Chilean Nitrates.

The Guano Islands.

The other stamp is that of a girl harvester and one wonders rather why they did not choose more up-to-date methods to illustrate their ideal. Hand broadcasting is not the latest method of applying manure, and during the hundred years that nitrate has been exported the farming methods have improved tremendously.

The other illustrated stamp comes from another South

American State—Peru—and pictures the Guano Islands for which this region of the coast is famous. It is rather unfortunate that the stamp is lithographed in one colour, it makes it very difficult to pick out the design properly. The stamp is really rather pretty, consisting as it does of a number of sea birds resting on the island, while there are also a number in the air, and on the horizon is a ship—hardly distinguishable were it not for the smoke.

The large sailing ship which takes up most of the central portion of the design from the Turks, and Caicos Islands is so attractive that one is very likely to miss the foreground, and as this shows a picture of salt-raking in progress, it is a pity that the ship—though pretty—takes away from the general interest.

These stamps are no longer in circulation. The design is a very pleasing one, and at the same time reminds us of the amount of sunshine that these islands must have in order to evaporate the water to produce such fine salt. It is said that these islands produce the finest salt in the world.

The Mining Prospector.

The stamp was issued in 1900 and in 1909 the design was changed. It is well worth scrutinizing this stamp very carefully, because there is something wrong about it.

The ship is an ocean-going sailing vessel, but the drawing shows it so close to the shore that a plank Way is seen for wheeling the salt on board.

TAKING a journey further north will enable us to think about the Unite d States of America. Man has always been ready to undergo great hardship in the search for gold and other precious metals, and owing to greed he generally likes to keep either to himself or have perhaps one partner. If one of a body of men, each feels that the sharing out will mean a personal loss.

Salt Ranking.

The Soar Basin.

In 1898 U.S.A. issued a set of stamps and on one of them is a picture of a Western Mining Prospector. The country round him does not look inviting and as the search for wealth must be a lonely task, one almost wants to congratulate the designer on giving the man a dog.

As a contrast to this peaceful, if lonely view, look at the stamp from the Saar Basin showing a view of the pit head at

Reding. By the Treaty of Versailles the coal fields of the Saar Basin were ceded to France for 15 years. This period is over next year, when the inhabitants are to decide by a plebiscite whether they will remain French, return to Germany, or become a self-governing community.

The set to which this stamp belongs was issued in 1921 and among the views shown may be mentioned the 40pf.—a view of the slag heap at Volklingen, the 1 m. with a wire rope railway.

ONE of the most curious stamp designs is that on the 28k. of Russia issued in 1929. The stamp shows a blast furnace on the right, while on the left is a graph, with three black lines showing the output of pig-iron for the years 1913, 1928, and 1933.

The last, of course, represents an estimation, because the stamp was issued four years before this date. The figure for 1928 represents the production at the beginning of the five-year plan, that for 1933 the result of this determined effort to stimulate production. The figures 4.2, 3.2 and 1.2 are millions of metric tons.

A Russian Chart.

SUMMER SPORTS ON STAMPS

IS stamp collecting a summer or a winter hobby? Ask most people and they will certainly say that it is a winter hobby pure and simple. In fact they will go so far as to say that the stamp album together with all accessories should be locked away throughout the summer. Then, when the winter comes, it is all the more interesting.

One could understand their argument, and perhaps agree with them if every post office in the world closed down for the summer, but letters are written and sent during the summer and new issues appear during all the year.

American Baseball.

The philatelist who closes down for the summer must miss an enormous amount, and if he tries to make up during the winter, he must then scamp a lot or else make a burden of his pleasure, for in philately one is wiser to make haste slowly. Even if the English weather was more definite and we could be certain of remaining out of doors throughout the summer days then we might put our stamps away and live in the open for the good of our health, but everyone knows how fickle our weather is, and unquestionably it is an excellent thing to have something to do when the rain falls.

From Bulgaria.

The Gladiators.

SUPPOSE we pass one of these wet afternoons with our stamp albums looking for summer sporting stamps?

Of truly summery aspect is the Bulgarian stamp, issued in 1931, one of a set of seven each depicting an event of the Balkan Olympic Games. Other values show fencing, cycling, gymnastics, football, horse riding, and the highest value the spirit of Victory, a figure with a laurel wreath and trumpet.

For the early issues of sports stamps we must turn to the pages of Greece, and here we shall find an issue dated 1896 commemorating the Olympic Games which were revived in that year and held at Athens.

These were the first of the Olympic Games as we now know them, though for the designs of the issue use was made of the ancient contests. For example, the stamp illustrated shows two gladiators, while another value shows a picture of a chariot race.

Luckily for us our sports are of a less serious nature than was the case in these ancient times and the stamp from the Philippine Islands shows a present day form of sport—a team game. Baseball certainly has its element of danger and this is plainly indicated in the stamp by the mask and other protection worn by the catcher.

If any readers have witnessed a baseball match they will realise why such protection is used, only it seems a little rough on the referee that he should have to wear the padding and the face mask that he does. Baseball is to the American what football is to us.

THE Portuguese stamp shown is interesting in that it almost amounts to a tax stamp. Curiously enough, this tax was only collected on certain days, and on those days one of these 15c. stamps had to be affixed to the mail in addition to the ordinary postage. If it was not, then one of the postage due stamps was used by the authorities to collect the amount due, together with the fine for not using the required stamp.

The stamp bears the date 1928 and the word "Amsterdao" at the bottom, so readers will not need to be told of what the fund was in aid: and those who are hurdlers will agree that the form of the hurdler shown on the 1930 stamp from Cuba is definitely better.

In 1932 Jugo Slavia issued a set of six stamps in connection with the European Rowing Championships and the specimen of this set illustrated shows a view of the river Danube at Smederevo. On other stamps there are different views with pairs, fours or eights.

The Portuguese Hurdler.

THIS must not be thought to be all the sports stamps. Very far from it. Every country in which the Olympic Games is held has an issue to commemorate these, so readers should look up the countries in which these events have been held and see what sports are illustrated on the stamps.

A Rower from Jugo-Slavia.

When the Games were held at Paris in 1924 France issued four but they were rather poor efforts, whereas in 1928 Holland gave us eight, six of which might be classed as summer games.

SPORTS

AT first sight one would hardly expect to be reminded of out-door recreations by one's stamp collection. Yet the importance of sport in international relations is now so great that a number of countries have depicted sporting events as the main theme of the design of their stamps.

Holland Sculling.

Tennis in the Phillipines.

Of course, some countries are always looking for subjects so that they can issue a new set of stamps, and such countries welcome anything as an excuse so that they can add to their revenue at the expense of philatelists. There are, however, what one might call a number of genuine sporting events which have been commemorated in this way.

Even the smallest collection will surely contain a specimen of a Grecian stamp showing a scene from the original Olympic Games. These were said to be founded in 776 B.C., and held every four years until 393 A.D., then they were abolished until the first (as we know them) was held at Athens in 1896, since then they have been held regularly except for 1916.

In 1924 France issued four stsmps in commemoration of the fact that the Olympic Games were held that year in Paris. Actually the designs did not show any particular sport in progress; the 10c being that of an athlete crowned with a wreath of laurel with his arm stretching over the Stadium, and with the Arc de Triomphe in the background. The other designs are even less sporting.

Holland in 1928 also issued stamps, eight in number, as an Olympic Games issue because the games were that year held at Amsterdam. These were sold at a premium which varied according to the value of the stamp, being 1c up to the 5c stamp, 2c for the 7 1/2, 10 and 15c and 3c for the 30c. The ssubjects of the stamps were:—sculling (illustrated), fencing, association football, yachting, putting the weight, running, horse-riding and boxing.

In 1932 when the Games were held at Los Angeles, the United States of America issued two stamps, one showing a sprinter 'On his mark' the second one of a discus thrower backed by a globe.

One very 'summery' stamp has been issued lately—the 6c. of the Phillipine Islands showing a tennis player. There are two other stamps in this issue and they depict a scene from a baseball game and a scene from a game of netball. These three stamps were in commemoration of the Tenth Far Eastern Games which were held at Manilla.

It is rather a good thing for us living in the west to know that those in the east are keen on sport. We are rather prone to think that we are the only nation which takes sport seriously. Another reminder of the summer is the 400 kr. of the 1925 set from Hungary. This particular stamp shows a man diving, whilst others in the set show scenes from ski-ing, skating, fencing, association football, scouting and hurdling.

A Rustic Goal!

Hurley in Ireland.

The set was issued in order to obtain funds for sport's associations, the stamps being sold at double face value. If you have one of these stamps in your collection and look at the back you will see printing on it, and the inscription gives the aforementioned information.

Lately Association football has been the subject of the design on a great number of stamps. This year Italy has issued three sets; one for ordinary postage, one for air mail, and one for her colonies, all in commemoration of the World football Championship. These three sets were prepared before the result was known, so it cannot be that Italy issued them to mark her victory. (Italy beat Czecho-Slovakia by 2—1 in the final).

Of the stamps which were issued the majority show some scene from football. The illustration above shows a player being tackled, but it rather looks as though the designer was not very sure of the game for the tackler appears as likely to receive a sprained ankle.

Perhaps the most curious football design is that on the stamp from Uruguay. In 1924 and again in 1928 the Uruguayan team won the contest in the Olympic Games, and a set of three stamps was issued. Appearing on each was a goal post, made of rustic wood, with the crossbar resting in the forks on the two uprights! And these all have branches and leaves sprouting from them, while in the middle of the crossbar a football is balanced. And on the ball a bird is perched!

The Irish Free State have now joined the list of countries which have depicted sports scenes. The 2d. stamp illustrated portrays a player in their national game of hurley. It is apparently a more strenuous game than hockey, however, as the stick is thicker, and the ball bigger.